ONE CAN MAKE A DIFFERENCE

You Can Make A Difference !

LS Keilbart

ONE CAN MAKE A DIFFERENCE

Written by
L. S. Keilbart

Illustrated by
Barbara Benson

JANUS PUBLISHING COMPANY LTD
London, England

First Published in Great Britain 2005 by
Janus Publishing Company Ltd,
105–107 Gloucester Place,
London W1U 6BY

www.januspublishing.co.uk

British Library Cataloguing-in-Publication Data
A catalogue record for this book
is available from the British Library

ISBN 978-1-85756-792-2

Cover Design: Barbara Benson
Printed and bound outside the UK

Tom was riding his bike in town. He rode to the city park where the children played. Tom had not been to the park in a very long time.

2

Tom wanted to play basketball with his friends, but the basketball court was littered with garbage. He was very sad. As he looked around he noticed that the whole park looked the same way.

Tom had a great idea. He and his friends could clean up the park today and play ball tomorrow. EVERYONE thought it was a great idea. EVERYONE helped.

The next day when they arrived at the park, they noticed it was dirty again. Pop cans were on the ground, newspapers were stuck to the fence and food containers had been dropped on the sidewalk and grass. NO ONE wanted to play.

Tom wanted to clean up again, but everyone said it was useless. It would just get dirty again tomorrow. EVERYONE left. Tom wanted to make the park clean again so he and his friends could play.

He went home and asked his Mom if he could have the big container in the garage. She asked him what he was doing. He told her he wanted to clean up the park. She agreed to let him take it.

12

Next, Tom asked his dad if he could borrow some white paint. Dad asked what he was doing. He told him that he wanted to clean up the park. Dad agreed to let him use it.

14

Tom found his sister, Sally, playing in her bedroom. Tom asked her if he could borrow her stencils. Sally asked what he was doing. He told her that he wanted to clean up the park. Sally let him use her stencils.

Tom's last item was tape. He found that in his room.

18

Tom took all of his items and began his project. First he spelled 'CANS' with Sally's stencils. Then he taped them to the container. He carefully painted across the word. He took the container to the park and placed it near the water fountain.

The next day Tom went back to the park. He noticed that people had been putting cans in the container. He knew it had made a difference.

Tom looked around the park again. He could see newspapers all along the fence. Tom knew the town had a recycling programme for paper. He thought the newspapers should be put in with other papers to be recycled.

24

Tom went across the street to City Hall. He asked for a paper recycle box. The clerk asked what he was doing. He told her he wanted to clean the park. She agreed to give him the box.

26

Tom put the box marked 'PAPER' near the water fountain. Afterwards, Tom went along the fence and gathered the newspapers. When he was done, he placed them in the box marked 'PAPER'. The park was looking better.

As Tom rode his bike home he thought about the food containers on the sidewalks and the grass. People liked having picnics at the park. He thought a dumpster would be the perfect answer.

30

In the morning Tom heard the garbage truck going down the street. Tom rode his bike after the truck until it stopped. He asked the garbage man for a dumpster to be placed in the park. The garbage man asked what he was doing. Tom told him he wanted to clean the park. The garbage man thought it was a good idea. He agreed to put one in the park.

32

Later that day, Tom went to the park and saw the dumpster in the corner of the park. What he did not see was cans on the ground, newspapers on the fence or food containers on the sidewalk or the grass. The park was finally clean!

Tom saw many people in the park today. More children were playing. More parents were talking. More squirrels were running. His friends were playing basketball. EVERYONE was having a good time.

36

ANYONE could have done it. EVERYONE had helped. NO ONE was left out. All it took was one person who wanted to make a difference.

38